CARNEGIE BUILDING
1 LaGrange Street
Newnan, GA 30263

TV, YES OR NO

Lin Picou

rourkeeducationalmedia.com

Scan for Related Titles
and Teacher Resources

Teaching Focus:

Endings- *ed* –*ing*- Locate the words watched and watching in the book. Write the words and underline the common root word. Then compare the endings. How does each ending change the meaning of the root word? Practice using the endings with another root word.

Before Reading:

Building Academic Vocabulary and Background Knowledge

Before reading a book, it is important to set the stage for your child or students by using pre-reading strategies. This will help them develop their vocabulary, increase their reading comprehension, and make connections across the curriculum.

1. *Read the title and look at the cover. Let's make predictions about what this book will be about.*
2. *Take a picture walk by talking about the pictures/photographs in the book. Implant the vocabulary as you take the picture walk. Be sure to talk about the text features such as headings, Table of Contents, glossary, bolded words, captions, charts/ diagrams, or Index.*
3. *Have students read the first page of text with you then have students read the remaining text.*
4. *Strategy Talk – use to assist students while reading.*
    - *Get your mouth ready*
    - *Look at the picture*
    - *Think…does it make sense*
    - *Think…does it look right*
    - *Think…does it sound right*
    - *Chunk it – by looking for a part you know*
5. *Read it again.*
6. *After reading the book complete the activities below.*

Content Area Vocabulary
Use glossary words in a sentence.
discussion
entertain
government
opponents
proponents
tempted

After Reading:

Comprehension and Extension Activity

After reading the book, work on the following questions with your child or students in order to check their level of reading comprehension and content mastery.

1. *How does watching TV affect us? (Summarize)*
2. *What are ways advertisements on TV affect us positively and negatively? (Asking questions)*
3. *How much TV do you watch each day? Is it harmful to you? Explain. (Text to self connection)*
4. *Why do you think people would rather watch TV shows about history or science instead of reading a book? (Asking questions)*

Extension Activity

How much TV do you watch? With the help of a grownup, record each show you watch and the length of each show for one week. Create a bar graph that shows how much TV you watch on each day of the week. Which day did you watch the most TV? Which day did you watch the least? What are some ways you can balance your screen time better?

Table of Contents

Introduction

"May I watch TV, Mom?"

"You watched two shows before school this morning. That's enough television for today."

When you discuss something with someone, you may not agree with each other.

Have you had this **discussion** at home? Should there be a limit on watching TV? Let's think about it.

Arguments for Watching TV

Proponents of television viewing argue that TV programs provide benefits. Interesting TV shows can give you something to talk about with your friends.

Your television can show you places where people look and speak differently than you.

Travel shows about different parts of the world can be a good way to learn about other cultures.

You can learn from the ways television characters create and solve problems.

Special channels can teach us about history, science, and **government**. They can also help us plan our day.

Let's check the weather channel before we plan our picnic!

Some families watch TV together, then discuss what they see.

Watching news shows informs us about world events, local events, and sports teams.

Concerts can **entertain** us and cooking demonstrations can introduce us to new foods.

Comedy shows can make us laugh and feel happy.

Television shows can entertain people who are in hospitals and nursing homes.

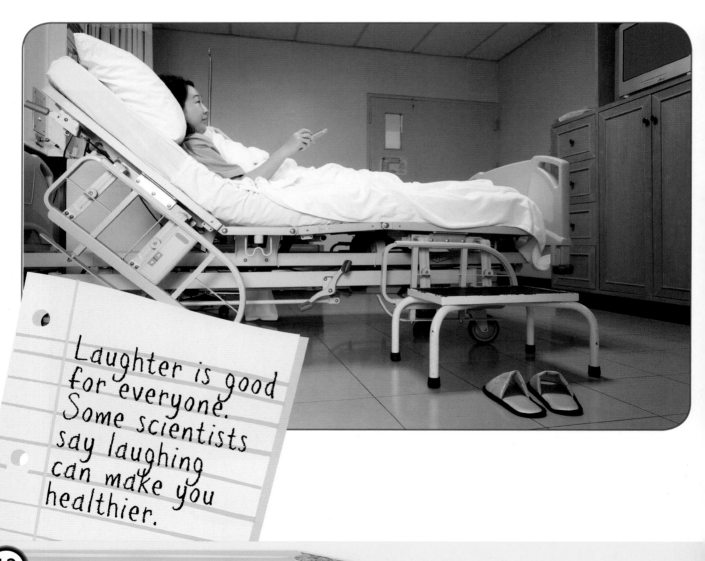

Laughter is good for everyone. Some scientists say laughing can make you healthier.

Arguments against Watching TV

Opponents of television viewing think that it is harmful. They argue that TV shows can sometimes make us feel sad or scared.

Some TV characters can be poor role models, sharing harmful or unhealthy habits.

Some shows and commercials can make us hungry for unhealthy foods.

Advertisements on television can make us want things we don't need.

Many of us sit most of the day at school or work, then are **tempted** to sit more and watch TV.

Watching TV shows can keep people from getting a healthy amount of exercise.

Some opponents say watching TV keep kids and adults indoors too much.

Watching television doesn't require people to use their imaginations like books and games do.

You Decide

There's a lot to think about before you grab the remote.

What is your opinion about watching TV? Share what you think by writing an opinion paper!

Writing Tips

— Tell your opinion first. Use phrases such as:
- *I like* _____.
- *I think* _____.
- _____ *is the best* _____.

— Give many reasons to support your opinion. Use facts instead of stating your feelings.

— Use the words *and, because,* and *also* to connect your opinion to your reasons.

— Explain your facts by using phrases, such as *for example,* or *such as.*

— Compare your opinion to a different opinion. Then point out reasons your opinion is better. You can use phrases such as:
- *Some people think,* _____ *but I disagree because* _____.
- _____ *is better than* _____ *because* _____.

— Give examples of the positive outcomes of someone agreeing with your opinion. For example, you can use the phrase: *If* _____ *then* _____.

— Include a short story about your own experiences with the topic. For example, if you are persuading someone that the best pet is a dog, you can talk about your pet dog.

— Restate your opinion so your reader remembers how you feel.

Glossary

discussion (dis-KUHSH-uhn): a conversation with a purpose, in which different opinions are expressed

entertain (EN-tur-TAYN): to amuse someone in an enjoyable way

government (GUHV-urn-muhnt): the system and people that govern a country or state

opponents (uh-POH-nuhnts): people on the other side of an argument

proponents (pro-POH-nuhnts): people who support something

tempted (TEMPT-ed): to appeal strongly to someone

Index

Show What You Know

1. When can watching TV make you happy?
2. Why are some characters poor role models?
3. How can you be active while watching TV?

Websites to Visit

www.nickjr.com/games

www.pbskids.org

www.games.com/educational-games

About the Author

Lin Picou has been teaching for 34 years. She has a master's degree in English Education from the University of South Florida. When she's not in the classroom, she rides her bike and plays baseball with her grandson, Evan.

Meet The Author!
www.meetREMauthors.com

www.rourkeeducationalmedia.com

PHOTO CREDITS: Cover (left): ©Dragon Images; Cover (boy): ©Gemenacom; Cover (girl): ©Pablo Hidalgo; page 1, page 7, page 9, page 11, page 14: ©jazzIRT; page 4: ©Tremayne Ward-Smith; page 5: ©Dereje Belachew; page 6: ©skynesher; page 7: ©brytta; page 7 (bottom), page 12 (bottom): ©rangepuppies; page 8: ©Pamela Albin Moore; page 9: ©Artistico, page 9, page 11: ©Yuri Arcurs; page 10: ©Christopher Futcher; page 12: ©Mavadee; page 13: ©princessdiaf; page 14: ©boggy22; page 15: ©Alena Ozerova; page 16: ©michaeljung@163.com; page 17: ©Susan Chiang; page 18: ©richywolf; page 19: ©Monkey Business Images; page 20 (left): ©Constantin Sinn; page 20 (right): ©LPETTET

Edited by: Keli Sipperley
Cover and Interior design by: Rhea Magaro

Library of Congress PCN Data

TV, Yes or No/Lin Picou
(Seeing Both Sides)
ISBN (hard cover)(alk. paper) 978-1-63430-345-3
ISBN (soft cover) 978-1-63430-445-0
ISBN (e-Book) 978-1-63430-544-0
Library of Congress Control Number: 2015931670

Printed in the United States of America, North Mankato, Minnesota

Also Available as:

ROURKE'S
e-Books